D0115776

PEACE RIVER

PEACE

RIVER

by

MICHAEL
WALTON

265
W A

Should we together
turn these pages,
let us turn them
lovingly. For
herein dwells an
Angel.

Herein, too, are
blessings Heaven
has given me to
share. Will you,
in trust, share
them?

thank Jacob and Leah Warner of the Boxwood Press, 116 Rosewood Drive, Greenbelt, Maryland 20770, U.S.A. for hand typesetting in Goudy Thirty with Goudy Initials; and Frederick W. Goudy for the typeface. I thank William Sessions, LTD., the Ebor Press, Huntington Road, York, YO3 9HS, England, for printing and binding. I thank the Artists: Vincent L. Fallon, Valerie Jacobs, and Frances Merrett.

✳ ✳ ✳ ✳ ✳

BRITISH LIBRARY CIP DATA
Walton, Michael
Peace River
1. Meditations
1. Title
242   BV4832.2
ISBN—0—9507000—0—2

✳ ✳ ✳ ✳ ✳

The book is MEDITATIVE and DEVOTIONAL;
It contains 33 Monotone Plates, and
1 in full colour.

✳ ✳ ✳ ✳ ✳

Peace River is Published by the Author at:
Melrose, 14 Clinton Rise, Beer,
E. Devon, EX12 3DZ, England.

✳ ✳ ✳ ✳ ✳ ✳ ✳

DEDICATED

in
gratitude
to all who,
knowing or
unknowing,
helped

PEACE RIVER

to birth.

eace River is an INNER
River; the River of Life,
the Divine Lifestream,
the Stream of Divine Healing.
Though to most of us invisible, it
is, none the less, most real. The
Author's earnest hope is that these
pages will bear testimony both to
its Sublime Reality, and practical
value. For Equity (balanced judgement), and Righteousness (upright
living), these are they that bring
the Peace of which Peace River
speaks. True Peace can only come

when they are present; they are,
therefore, essential to fulfil the
purpose of
       Peace River.

ND the Angel said to me, "You must allow yourself to be lifted up above contention." That implies there is somewhere contention is not. It is my purpose in this book to find that place and abide there.

RCHÆOLOGY tells us of long, long ago. Long again before that ancient time, a time which was a nadir in the experience of this Earth as a Soul System, was the Golden Age. The Soul, that is the body we carry with us from life to life, that part of us which is of the Eternal with its 'many mansions' and its power to infuse our here and now, was most radiant then, in the Golden Age or Age of Beauty. All was lovely, and the DIVINE GOODNESS reigned. There was no war, and the Earth herself was volatile. The Fall brought fixity and fear, and other evils too. It came about through certain wrong choices made by High Potentates who thought they knew better than GOD. Now, in these days, a wonderful Message has been brought to us from the High Heavens to show us the way back to the Golden Age, to show us how to put right the mistakes made, and regain our ancient and beautiful

Estate. To those who caused the Fall, explanation has been given. They are aware of their mistake, and are doing everything they can to put it right. Angels, Archangels and Gods rally round to help them and us. It is a stupendous Drama, the Drama of the Return. We are called to help, and the reflections contained in this book are an attempt to enable us to see some at least of the many ways we can help. The Message to which I and others owe so much, which is in

itself like a wonderful Stream or
River, was brought to us by the
Rev. J. Todd Ferrier, and the reader
would do well to turn to his
writings for full and deep Unveilings
on these subjects. His books are
obtainable from: The Literature
Secretary, The Order of the Cross,
10 De Vere Gardens, Kensington,
LONDON W8 5AE.

The debt owed by the present
writer to the inspiration given by
these writings and by those who
have made them a part of their

lives, is incalculable. The Homeland
of which they bear witness is filled
with a sweetness never cloying
and a beauty unalloyed.

Book 1

THE
RIVER

HERE is within Man an inborne urge to search, whether for gold or for knowledge; and to explore, whether it be Antarctica, Mars, or the Golden Age. The search for and exploration of the Golden Age, with which we are here concerned, involves us in the rediscovery of many things WITHIN US forgotten for untold Ages. It involves us in finding again our insight; for the Golden Age was the Age of the Soul, and it has again dawned on

Earth. It needs a reorienting of
our thinking, for values will change
as horizons widen. Indeed, it is our
WHOLE life needs turning again
Godward in all its many depart-
ments. A few of these we will
consider in the following pages,
and endeavour, with the help of the
Angels who ever minister to us, to
find again some of the Treasures
of the Soul. For, longtime since,
in the Days of the Golden Age of
yore, we all knew these Treasures
of Soul Knowledge. As we slowly

reawaken at the Dawn of this New
Age, these same Angels will impart
to us what we can receive. It is
with this enrichment we all go
onward, and rejoice.

HE history of this Earth, since the Fall of Man plunged it into chaos, has been inwrought with sadness. We would, with the magic Rod of DIVINE LOVE and POWER, endeavour to change the sadness to Joy. Coming up for healing in these days are the results of misunder-standings which Souls have had, one with another, during the Aeons of sorrow. In the past these have led to conflict and hurt. There will be those we meet in the way with whom we have had these unhappy relationships. In these days the DIVINE LOVE will draw us together, the hurts will be tenderly unveiled, and the nature of past conflicts revealed. We are expected to be brave and sensible; to bless the hurts, and allow the conflicts to be healed. It is not easy. Many things get in the way. Our prayers will be for willingness to listen, also to see, and to focus our seeing. It is always a help to observe how the DIVINE LOVE works. There is never ever any blame or criticism for our having given hurt or caused conflict. Although we were often the victims of circumstances which in our darkness we may even have brought about, we do have, and rightly, to bear the responsibility of putting them right, and rejoice to do so—it is after all but a small thing relative to the Solar mishap—and follow faithfully the Path of Restitution. This lovely word, when we go back to its origin (Latin Statuere), we see is concerned with that which is to stand erect. This is our return to an uprightness in all walks of life.

FTEN in our pathway
through life we come
upon situations laden
with false traditions, or rather,
traditions, which for some reason
or other have become overlaid with
falsity, having originally been
inspirations of the DIVINE. Two
examples out of many would be the
Caste System in India, and, in Scot-
land, the System of Clans. Wonderful in their original concept, much
hurt was wrought in and through
both, because of misdirection of

power. Healing can sometimes be accomplished by a return to the original concept. However, in instances where decay had gone too far, complete removal of the edifice might be the only possible cure. The wonderful vision lying behind the Caste System concerned the understanding and application of Hierarchy in Government, and the ordering of a true freedom in Social Life. The understanding of the Clan System, its Divine origin, its purpose in teaching

us the nature of a sacrificial love
as this is to be exemplified in a
heaven-inspired family life, and the
relationships of families one with
another in an upright, balanced,
and constructive peace, is a need
deeply pressing upon us in these
days. To look at the triumphs,
and also the sad failures of these
Systems, will help us in our search
after a true Divinity and its
manifestation.

HEN we are faced with that curious phenomena, the inhibition. We would, through a prayerful quest, seek a sane attitude. It may be that there is inherent in some inhibitions a true cover or defence of a sensitive part of our make-up. And yet, how often do inhibitions cause us to miss out on the spontaneity of life! It would seem one needs to be watchful that an inhibition is doing a needful service to ourselves or others. Probably by the time we

see it in ourselves it is time it
was thrown away, or replaced by
something better!

OLLOWING this thought we notice that, about the time Europe was becoming the scene of that great flowering of architecture which resulted in the Norman Churches and Cathedrals we love to contemplate today for their nobility and Godwardness, there were armies flourishing as de-fenders of the Faith. These had begun at the time of the First Crusade, a venture filled with deep spirituality though later sadly misdirected. These armies were led by Knights, deeply spiritual men and a few women, members of religious Knightly Orders, held by vows to defend, save, or rescue Christendom from the various evils of the time. However debased these Orders became, it is helpful to remember the purity and sanctity of their origins. Also, for our particular purpose here, the nature of the Armour the Knights wore. For, like the wonderful architectural edifices which spoke of Man's soaring aspirations, so this Armour spoke of his Soulic defences. It was a direct result of inward vision which produced it, many ages previous, and, though misapplied —the sword of the Spirit, for example, becoming a carnal weapon — reminds us, if we allow it, of the way we can as Souls take on a spiritual and truly protective armour. This will help enable us to become again the generating stations from which to radiate the Light of Truth into the World, while at the same time protecting us from the backflow of evil. It can be described as an atmosphere surrounding our life, an atmosphere of Radiance which has the action of a valve, allowing that Radiance of Heaven to shine forth through us, but nothing evil to flow back in. The various parts of that Armour speak to us in a concrete way of this atmosphere which, through prayer, meditation, and application in life's deeds, we would ever seek to engender within and around our life, and all whom we love and cherish.

AY we consider the place of Limitation in our lives, for though, inevitably, in a fallen world it has its falseness too, and one needs to look carefully at things which do limit us to see if they are true, yet there are some most wonderful examples of its essential place in the Universe and in our own experience. We are, all of us, under true limitation, and it is helpful to remember that that is always benefic. I suppose that in the world of physical phenomena the best example is that of a river, which, but for the presence as a limiting factor of its bed and banks would not be a river at all. Again, our own physical body. Without the considerable pressure on us of 15 lbs per square inch we would not be a body at all but simply elements dispersed. The river is a beautiful thought on which to reflect. A slow, deep, solemn river flowing. Or a frisky, rollicking, bounding over stones kind of rivulet. The waterfall. The still

pool. One will relate these to life. The music of their varied flow and stillness adding up to a symphony of living, the Symphony of
Peace River.

ROBABLY few subjects have inherent within them the possibility of so much peace-bringing, as the understanding of different religions and their essential oneness. It would ever be our edeavour to find this oneness and live it, for surely the Peace of Mankind depends largely upon this. In the seventh century T'ang dynasty in China we find a remark-able instance of this. Buddhism, long accepted, Mohammedan and Christian Emissaries were received

by the Taoist Emperor Li Shih Min
(T'ang T'ai Tsung, 600-649 A.D.).
He not merely welcomed them, but
gave full scope of activity, and
even aid to build Mosques and
Churches. It is more than probable
that, had followers of Zarathustra
and Mani also sent envoys, they
too would have received like wel-
come, as indeed they did some
years later. Whether he did or did
not actively participate in their
worship I do not know. Yet the
peaceful coexistence of these

several principles within his own
bosom, and therefore within the
bosom of his People, is indeed
wonderful. Surely a salutory
example to all Mankind.

ONCERNING the true reading of phenomena. Surely many of the mistakes we make are because of a tendency to read results rather than causes. Causes are so much more difficult to see. Indeed, often, without the eyes of Angels, impossible. Apparent impossibility of finding these eyes has misled devout men and women to atheism. But they ARE there, these wonderful inner eyes. For the Angel Man within, and the Angel Woman, too, are

awaiting our rediscovery of powers
by the use of which we may
penetrate the veils and see again
the great truths lying behind all
phenomena, whether of world
history or the history of a Race;
the mineral kingdoms or the
kingdoms of nature; or the ofttimes marred visage of Souls.

ROPHETS have seen angels. Do we sometimes ask ourselves, "Who were they; those Seers and Prophets of eld; why and how so gifted, why so downtrodden, persecuted, and misunderstood?" Can we, too, develop within us the capacities which so distinguished their lives? These and cognate questions are surely most natural, and utterly in harmony with our endeavour toward a true lowliness and humilty. For these capacities are aspects of

the Godhood within Man, and in
Humility, to be sought for, found
again, and cultivated.

T IS unfortunate that, largely because of a lack of wholeness in our thinking, we have come to view religion and science as incompatible. To write of these two great areas of Man's endeavour together is not easy, for terminology developed by both has tended to divide rather than unite. Research is a common practice of the Scientist; well would it be for the true Mystic if he approached a rediscovery of the Kingdom of Heaven through this avenue. Blind faith has, in the eyes of science, stigmatised the Mystic; well for him when he discovers for himself this mote in his own eye and removes it. A truly soulic illumination, resulting from the opening of the inner eyes of Man, will immeasurably aid the Scientist in his earnest search for Truth. May the day hasten when science and religion are seen as twin aspects of the Divine Wholeness, complementing and aiding each other, both in inward illumination

and the practical outward application
of Truth.

F THE many fine Orders of Monasticism which grew up at the time of the great Cathedrals and the Mystic Armour and have flourished since, there is one only which concerns us here. It is one that is available to us all. The word monastic means 'living alone.' In this strict sense it really applies only to the Hermit. For monasticism generally a more apt definition would be 'living apart.' A true apartness is just that which enables us to Live. We work and function on Earth, but our strength comes from Heaven. The aim of the traditional Orders was to bring that apartness in fact, and separate men and women in earthly houses and from the outer world. The kind to which we set our vision is one where that separateness is of the Soul (the feminine or soul element in Man) from the outer life. Then the lifting up above outer conflict of every living part of us. It is only in this way that, truly above our task, like the axe above the

wood block, we can effectually
accomplish it.

ATER we shall write more concerning criticism and its true place in the Redeemed life. From time to time, counsel has been offered with regard to self-criticism. One has been advised to turn the criticism one may feel for another on to oneself, for, it is said, criticism for another stems from thinking one sees error in them, whereas it is mostly a reflection of oneself one sees. Although this may be true, indeed in many instances probably is so, to turn the criticism on to oneself is no cure. Indeed it merely tends to the destruction of ones own atmosphere. Self-criticism is no less destructive than any other form; only its direction is different. May we remember at all times that GOD NEVER EVER CRITICISES US. He sees in us always the Goodness, the Beauty, the Truth and Nobility of HIMSELF. With these He gently aids us to take up the broom of purity and sweep clean the whole of our Temple. In our impoverishment

He gives us nourishment; in our
weakness, strength. Although He
asks of us our ALL, He never
expects more than at any time we
can give.

IVINE Healing is not a vague and woolly thing as some would have it. Based on Divine Law, and the application of that Law, it is in every aspect truly scientific and practical. It concerns the making WHOLE again of our Life. In science we speak of polarisation—the horizontal and vertical polarisation of a wave, for example. Also, the situation where light waves emanate haphazardly from a centre; that is nonpolarised light. Polarisation concerns the Healer of today, too, for there are many instances in the Soul Life and functioning where elements of the soul's constitution are nonpolarised. In the Science of Being, or the understanding of Man's Soulic superstructure, we have to learn how these elements are to be brought back to a state of upright-ness (vertical polarisation) and balance (horizontal polarisation), thus helping to make us again

WHOLE.

F we turn to magnetism we find possible a similar comparison as that in the preceding section. A metal which is fully magnetised has its atoms laid in order and facing all in the same direction. This is also true of the elements of the Soul which is in accord with, and responsive to, the magnetic pull of the Heavens. This is so also of our thinking and feeling. One says one is magnetically attracted to a subject; one's thoughts are aligned towards it.

One is magnetically attracted to
another human being; something
comes toward one electrically and,
because our elements are rightly
aligned, there is a response, we are
drawn together. Our hopes and
prayers are toward an awakening
within us of the magnetic pull of
the Heavens, as this relates to the
reorienting of our own life and our
relationships with Souls. When we
are willing, the Gates of the Eternal
World will open to us and draw
us together there, thus holding

the WHOLE of our life in absolute
safety.

ANY words there are in our language indicating the centripetal mode of functioning, the inflowing, in contrast to the centrifugal or outflowing. One only has to think of a few,—recreate, rejuvenate, inspire, aspire for example—and many more will come to mind. I mention this because from time to time one is confronted with "why pray," or "why meditate, why worship." All these are, in the first instance, concerned with the inflow of our powers, and it is important we try to understand just why it is needful. In some contexts it is so obvious; in others far less so. For example, no-one would think of trying to chop a block of wood without first lifting up the axe. Yet how many of us try to crack the husk of a problem without first going 'up' inwardly. Or, imagine one has never before seen an archer using his bow. Knowing the arrow was to travel forward, to see him first draw it back would appear curious, to say the least. Many of us have forgotten our pristine spirituality and the nature of a truly centripetal or inward approach to life. We have, perforce, had to function (mal-function, rather) on this poor topsy turvy planet for so long without any real opportunity or possibility of Soulic respiration that, now it is once again available, those parts of our makeup needed to avail themselves of it have partly atrophied, like an athlete's muscles

unused for a decade. In a most real
sense we have again to take this
inward journey back to our Source,
the realm at once of our origin,
our Home, our inspiration, where
we can again find the true and
sustaining Soulic air to breathe,
and the light which illuminates all
things. For to fully aspire physically
we need pure air. To aspire Soulicly
we need atmospheres nutritive and
exhilarating to the Soul.

e HAVE written of the Soul. This Soul of ours has a memory, dulled to the point of forgetfulness in most of us by the Fall. When her memory is reawakened we shall realize that this present life of ours is like a tiny drop—a very important drop, certainly—in the ocean of time. Important, because we can use it for much good. Tiny, because of the vast flung ages which surround the Soul; yet these Eternities she has built up into the fabric of her

Life. It is because of this that we can essay to take the spiritual Journey set out in the third part of this book, the Journey to our Homeland. Where is this Homeland? It is, in the first place, within us. Yet some there are who, in their Soul life, are not natives of this planet. For some their Home will also be in the Solar Body, and they can journey to it in consciousness even whilst living here. Thus, we have two Homes, intimately related.

e see, amid the hills and mountains of our native land, the Earth's rivers. We rejoice in the joy they bring us. We rejoice, too, that they remind us of Peace River, the inner River of Life. This ministers to our Soul needs. Life cannot be without water. Mystically, water is a symbol of Truth. But the River of Life, or the Divine Lifestream, is more than this. It contains within it the very substance and Essence of Life itself.

It is the Mystic Bread and Wine,
the living flowing stream which is
also full of colour and music; for
these, too, nourish the Soul. The
greater our aspiration the more
fully we move into this wonderful
Stream of Living Substance, the
more our Life takes on its beauty
and its strength. Having thus made
our life one in and with it, it can
be caused to flow through us to
Souls and to the World.

INTERLUDE

—◆—

GRACE

HERE have been many
forms of Grace.
Many supplicate.
The blessing of GOD flows
to and around us
continually.
There is no need to supplicate.
He bids us become
aware.

These are
GRACES OF VERITY:
They affirm things true.

HE Sun and the Earth
have given for
our nourishment
their glory.

May our hearts
be filled with
thankfulness
and
peace.

⟨⟨⟨⟩⟩⟩ ⟨⟨⟨⟩⟩⟩ ⟨⟨⟨⟩⟩⟩

HE peace which we
hold in our hearts
is the silent
language of our
gratitude for Life
and for nourishment.

The peace which we
hold in our hearts
is the gratitude we
wing back to HIM
Who Created all
Life and all nourishment.

eace be upon us:

Peace flow through us:

Peace be unto all
who prepared the
food;
and
Peace dwell in
the food.

UR table is an
Altar, the food
upon it a
Symbol.

While the substance
of the food doth
sustain our
outer body,
may the reality of which
that symbol speaks
feed our Soul.
AMEN.

Book II

THE SOUL

AS A

SHIP

UPON THE

RIVER

HE Soul is a Ship upon the River of Life. She has her Being living within the Divine Lifestream; she bathes in the atmospheres of the River of Divine Healing. She is so fashioned that she is BUOYANT. As she flies up and down the river, responsive to the Heavenly zephyrs, she plies her trade 'twixt the Heavens and the Earth. This is the trade of all Lovers of GOD; they fructify the Earth life anew with the Sunshine of the Gods.

EACE River is flowing unto
us full of healing. Are we
able to accept it, and
enter into the Life it gives? We talk
of being a PATIENT. Do we think
much about PATIENCE? Even should
we do so, do we CONTEMPLATE this
activity? We might even ask ourselves, are we patient contempla-
tively, for surely that is coming
near to the meaning of patience;
an active and trustful waiting upon
the Heavens to touch us unto
PERFECT health and healing. We

do well to remember those beloved angels who ALWAYS help us. They, and the Heavenly Hosts, can only help us fully when we become RESPONSIVE. In our contemplative patience may we meditate upon our RESPONSE, and all that that beautiful word means.

NE of the essentials to a true inner equilibrium is ATMOSPHERE. How do we create an atmosphere, a beautiful atmosphere? We first of all, if we are wise, remember our Upper Room. It is wonderful, even in the busiest thoroughfares of life, how potent even the most fleeting recollection of it is. Speed on Earth, of earth-bound thought or sub-stance, is as nought to the speed of the flight of the Spirit in prayer to its Source, its Centre. Even the word re-collect is indicative of gathering oneself up and back to a focal point. This flight, even though it be momentary, brings the wing-beats of angels very close and begins to create a good atmosphere, a joyful, happy atmosphere. What-ever the need may be, an atmos-phere thus begun will always tend to find the POSITIVE aspect of things. If something unlovely is around us, at once LOVELINESS will begin to be apparent; something unharmonious, the HARMONIOUS will

come near and show itself. This is
the truth lying behind magic, and
the results often are truly 'magical,'
coming right through into the
outer life.

HOSE healing streams magically caught in that fleeting moment are ponderable when we have a placid, longer time. Such contemplative activity will strengthen our capacity to 'tune in' to the Heavenly Streams. They are like a Stream of Living Gold. Gold is the Symbol of Divine Love, and, before the Fall, was not fixed and solid as it now is, but volatile. This is not easy to understand, but the more we ALLOW ourselves to enter this

Stream of Living Gold, the more
we become aware of it as an
ATMOSPHERE surrounding us, full of
healing balm.

Stream of Living Gold from the High Heavens! Be thou my Canopy and Shield! Be thou my Chariot wheels and flying steeds, carrying me up in heavenly flight to the Celestial Pastures! I would now flee unto the Hills of GOD within me and partake of the nourishment there reserved for the Gods;—that is, the Godlike powers within me as a Child of Heaven;—that nourishment which fits me for life and service here.

e WOULD learn to know and affirm the Power from on High which is given to all things GOOD, TRUE and BEAUTIFUL, to triumph completely over their opposites. This is so with ALL things Godlike. Though there will be difficulties and sore trials ahead, we do have the ABSOLUTE ASSURANCE that GOOD WILL triumph, is triumphing. The "Divine Triumph is assured." What wonderful Affirmations these are! What wonderful Affirmations upon which to ponder!

e NEED, do we not, to build such truth into the very fabric of our Being so that it is with us day and night; every moment of every day, every moment of every night. Gradually, as we do this, we shall become strong in our lowliness, strong in our gentleness and peacefulness; strong in our forgiveness and our forbearance; strong in all things which help even the very outermost parts of our life heavenward. May our TRUST be even in the ALL-Triumphing One

GOD Who is our Healer. Because
He is our MAKER. He it is alone
can Heal us.

HEN we pray we essay to enter our Inner, Upper Room. Why should we do this? What should we expect to find there? This sacred hallowed Shrine is the centre of our Life, whether we are dwelling on these outer planes of the Planet Earth, or elsewhere. Because it is the centre it is the place best suited to INTIMATE communion with our MAKER. Of course He is everywhere, EVERYWHERE! In the tiny flower, the beautiful stone, the tree,

the mountain, the river, the mighty sea; just EVERYWHERE! You say, But how can GOD, the All-Good, be in Evil? He was and is the Original Good, of which the Evil is an inversion; the Beauty, Truth and Love of which ugliness, falsity and hate are the subversions. It is thus that He is everywhere, that all things good, true and beautiful Glorify HIM. But our RECOGNITION of HIM must become first at our own Centre, for that is where He presents HIMSELF most OPENLY. As it is the Place He made first for His dwelling within us when He Created us in His Likeness, so is it the Place of all places most sacred to Him. We may say, O, but I feel nearest to God when I'm playing football, or running or swimming, etc. Surely that is only because, though we may not be thinking it consciously, we are in fact, in the sheer enjoyment of whatever activity we are at the time employed, embodying Him Who is the All-Joyful One. That

we carry that joy and the atmosphere of that joy into the streams
of our activities, is the testimony
of our growing awareness of GOD's
Radiant PRESENCE at the Centre
of our Life, even in our Inner,
Upper Room.

HE Soul, in origin, is perfect. It is Divine. This affirmation of Truth is comforting, though not in a soft, lax way, for we have to work back to the realization of it—we have to make it again REAL for all to see. But it is comforting as an assurance that at the centre of our life, the centre of the Planetary Life, the centre of the Solar System and of all Systems and Galaxies, is a GOD of LOVE, a GOD Who CARES, a GOD Who is Omnipotent

and Omniscient, a GOD Who is now
in this very day, hour, moment,
loving ALL His Creation back to
uprightness and purity, gentleness
and peace. Notwithstanding
the chaos and suffering we see,
which is here only because wrong
choice was made—choice must be
free; we must be free to choose to
respond to the Way of the Heavens
or to our own way—ALL IS being
put right, because GOD is PERFECT
and made us so.

AYBE the best way to see this rectification of our ways is to envisage a situation where our own choice in a given instance is the same as the influence playing upon us from GOD. Then our will will be the same as HIS. It is so wonderfully spontaneous when it comes! So buoyant is the life and so joyous! In response to the beautiful, the loving, the Soul's choice just is the same as the heavenly — the same atmospheres breathed, the same 'manna' eaten, the same prayers prayed: —oh, and it is the absolute antithesis of dull! Some think, alas, to do heaven's will is just passive obedience. Surely nothing could be further from the truth! Is it not our active creative choosing and willing, likes and longings, which are to be influenced and then gradually polarised in accord with the vast Universal Life, the Motion of the Stars, the wonderment of the Soul in its contemplation of Galaxies upon Galaxies of the Creative Cosmos?

I often feel that, did we but realise our nearness in Soul consciousness say to a great world like that glorious star Arcturus, we should get our Soul perspective truer. The magnetism which irresistibly draws us to these great Homes of Souls is the magnetism which heals us here. It is the same magnetism which on a lower plane, orders and realigns the atoms in a magnet. The same magnetism which on the Soul level, reorients the Elements, the wonderful Mystic

Elements of which our Soul as a Sanctuary for the indwelling of the MOST HIGH is built up. It is that same magnetism which causes us to remember our Childhood, our Childlikeness to HIM Who is our FATHER and MOTHER in ONE, be-cause our CREATOR, the FASHIONER of our life. The magnetism which acts on the Upright of our life helps it, when it is deflected by the chaos in the world, to get back to its 'true.'

e WOULD be filled with Won-
der! Wonderment is the
Crown of Childlikeness;
Crown of true simplicity. Were we
more often filled with real wonderment we would find it opening the
doors and windows of our Soul,
enabling us to reach out to vaster
vistas of Life. It is just this capacity
to expand our vision which is so
useful when faced with such a ques-
tion as, "Who lives on Sirius?" Would
GOD really, think you, have taken
the trouble to make so marvellous

a Star as Betelgeux merely to revolve inanimate? Surely, commensurate with its radiance would be the Radiance of the Beings living there? Do they care for us? Methinks, when next we come to 'tune in' to our friend Arcturus, we shall be moved to tears of healing sorrow by the loving concern they who live there bear towards us. May we, as we rise up out of the Night of the Soul and greet again the Dawn—the Dawn of the Day in which they ever live—, remember

their loving care for us. They
shone through all our Aeons of
darkness; they shone to win us
back Home, to the Home and
Homeland of which we shall
write further on.

T IS our prayer, our Soul desire, that we allow ourselves to be lifted up. Looking into the star-like heart of a flower we see a tiny miniature of the Mystery of Life. We would have our attitude toward one another, our work and our play, become ever more beautiful. We would release ourselves from those things which weigh us down. Taking the flight of the Spirit to the pure air of heaven, we would know the rejuvenation flight gives, and the balm of the air. May it be that the eye salve of the heavens enables us, as indeed in time it will, to see again the wonderful colour, the living colour which is real substantial nourishment to our Soul; to hear again the grand choiring of Angelic throngs, and the Soul stirring symphonies. These, and the ORIGINAL of every true Art and Culture are the Trade of the Soul, those Mystic Orient riches she carries Earthward to enrich and purify, heal and redeem back the

Earth to her pristine Golden Age
Beauty.

INTERLUDE

ON

PRAYER

RUE Prayer lifts us up
above ourselves.
That is to say,
it lifts us up to
our best selves,
for:—
GOD lives in our
best selves,
Our best selves
in GOD.

HE purpose of prayer
  is:——
Not to propitiate
  an unheeding GOD,
Rather move and motivate
  our own earthly clod
To better things.

He purpose of prayer
is to bring
that which is
of the above,
and let it
permeate
all things.

AY we uplift our hearts
to the heavens within us,
that they be chalices for
the receiving of Love's
blessings.

MAY we carry in the
chalice of our hearts
the blessing of Love's
peace, and distribute
it through all the
ways of our going.

Book III

THE

JOURNEY

HE APPROACH to this
Journey, like the approach
to the ancient Cathedrals
over the greensward skirting them,
is gentle. Upon this greensward are
laid aside the outer cares and ways.
Upon it is PREPARATION made to
enter the Holy Place. Preparation
through purification of the Life and
reverent Approach, become the
Soul. Self-denial is concerned with
purification of ALL the Living
Temples of Life; sacrifice, with
making every act SACRED. The Will

in its final surrender is NOT will-less
nor weak. Rather is it, because
attuned to its Source and polarised
in Goodness and Truth, will-FULL;
that is to say, filled with GOD's
Will, responsive, resilient, and
strong. The Self is not something
to be cut away from us; rather is
it a part much needed, to be
oriented back to GOD, that He
HIMSELF may shine through us.
Oriented back, but in no false piety.
Oriented back that Self, or Persona,
may become a fit channel for the

Living Stream of Peace River. Self
is a garment which is to become
again Radiant. It is a garment
through which the Regal Gems of
Lowliness and Humility shine.

THE

JOURNEY

— ◆ —

A

MEDITATIVE SEQUENCE

IN

FOUR PARTS

WITH AN

ENVOI

O MEDITATE is to listen
to the Heavens within
us and reflect them in
everything we do.

VERY paragraph is a part of the sequence; each is, in itself, complete. To commune with oneself upon a single idea seen in a few words; to pause between thoughts; to contemplate. To focus, and be STILL.

OD IS HERE.

May we become
aware of this.

He bids us know
His peace, the
Peace which stills
all storms to
REST.

s we take leave of our earth tasks, we withdraw gently, blessing them, and expressing our appreciation of them, recognising that they are a true part of the wholeness of Life. Outwardly we leave them awhile. We go to renew contact with the Source of

ALL LIFE.

✳ ✳ ✳

s we seek to rise into
the Heavens within us
we wish to quieten
any false criticism
which may be present,
any fear, doubt, or
blame. These have no
place in the Life of the
Heavens, therefore
must have no place
here.

✳ ✳ ✳

HE ofttimes overactive
and falsely critical
mind, which has a
tendency to cut into and
across the Streams of
Divine Healing, needs to
be loved back to still-
ness and encouraged to
LISTEN.

HE atmospheres of quietude and stillness will help the healing streams draw near. In them we can come again to see the good in all Souls and the beautiful in everything, and recognise the PRESENCE of GOD with us.

e WOULD engender the quality of TRUST to replace fear and doubt; and ask that the true inner Fire rain down and consume away all blame. Thus, gradually, every part of our Life becomes responsive to the Divine Touch. It then becomes receptive to the Divine Power, which, from on High, SUSTAINS US, moves within us, and bears us HOME.

❧ ❧ ❧

e ARE transported
by the sustaining
Power of the
Divine Love.
We would realise
this. We are
moved by HIM
and gently
AWAKENED.

✼ ✼ ✼

e WOULD know
ourselves transported
to the Divine centre
within us, realising His
sustaining PRESENCE
with us now and
always. We would
further know His
Motion within us
and dwell with it,
for it is this which
awakens us to our
Ancient Estate.

❧ ❧ ❧

T is the turning point of the year. There are many turning points in a year. This was written between the Old and the New. The moment reminds us that, in the Cosmic sense, it is the turning point for MAN. He now turns again HOMEWARD.

✳ ✳ ✳

HE PATH HOME is
indicated by
SIGNPOSTS. These
were turned awry at
the time of the Fall.
We ask to be illumined
by GOD and reoriented;
then follow the
corrected inscriptions,
turn ourselves around,
and go HOME.

❊ ❊ ❊

e ASK to receive
Grace whereby our
Return Home shall
be accomplished.
It has to be within
ourselves first;
then its effects
can flow through
us.

✳   ✳   ✳

e FURTHER ask that
we may know true
gratitude. Gratitude
is full of grace;
they come from
the same root. Grace
is a Divine influence;
it regenerates,
it sanctifies,
it gives strength
to endure.

AY it be
our portion
to be filled
with heavenly Grace
and Gratitude
now and
	evermore!

❧ ❧ ❧

e RECOGNISE that all
things needful for our
journey are provided
by and gifted to us
from the ONE GOD,
the All-Beautiful,
the All-Bountiful,
the All-Loving,
FATHER-MOTHER.

HE word TURN reminds us of the CROSS. It is a Cross of Light. Its first letter is this Cross, t. The second is a cup, u. The word has within itself an URN. The Cross of Light and the Cup are ourselves, for we are made in GOD's Image.

※ ※ ※

UR Cup, the Cup of our Life has, because of the Fall, been turned away from its source and misused, used for wrong, even evil purposes. We ask for willinghood—that is, the realisation of willingness—for it to be turned back again and used for true purposes. May Grace fill us that we be helpful in this process.

✻ ✻ ✻

O TURN is also to fold. When we pray, we fold up. We seek also to be enfolded by the One Who is the Source of our Life. We have been away from HIM for a long time; we wish now to RETURN and RESIGN ourselves to HIM.

✳ ✳ ✳

HIS is another part of the meaning of TURN, to RESIGN unto in the sense of committal. We would also endeavour to turn adversity to good account, wondering how the heavenly Ones use our shortcomings to help us back Home; how they take our weakness and make of it strength. May we, if it be good for us, become aware how this is done, and both now and in the future be more helpful to those who try to help us.

※ ※ ※

HE results of such AFFIRMATION and PRAYER are manifold; they are a measure of our response. We need to remember that true prayer is always answered, though not necessarily, if made specific, in the way expected.

✻ ✻ ✻

OMMITTAL of the Life
for the service of the
Risen Christ — that
is, the Christ Life
arisen within us — will
bring responsibilities.
These will be many
and varied. An example
would be a request
from GOD to be full of
Divine Love and
Wisdom, and give
these to Souls.

✳ ✳ ✳

e KNOW and affirm that
the GREAT LOVE
always triumphs, even
though, for the fulfill-
ment of this, time may
be needed. May we
embody this affirma-
tion in our lives,
becoming aware that
GOD IS triumphing in
this very hour through
us.

✽ ✽ ✽

EEKING to become yet more fully aware of both the Overshadowing and the Undershadowing of the Divine Love, we would realise that out from the Fount of all Life, even from the Eternal World itself, is poured the Lifegiving Stream. Carried to us in the Divine URN it is poured into our own Cup as we lift this up. For we ourselves are the Vessels entrusted with this Lifestream; it is our Risen selves that both can and must carry it into the world.

✻ ✻ ✻

ow that in our degree
we have risen to and
are dwelling upon the
Planes of Heaven
within us, we can
listen to the Call of
the Inner Worlds and
receive the Benison of
the GREAT LOVE.

e HAVE, like a flower, opened to the sun-shine, His Sunshine. Thus hath He blessed us, by shining upon us with the Sunshine of His Love.

HE nature of His blessing of us is that He has us always in His keeping. Our remembrance of this is the measure of our THANKSGIVING.

eeking to be conscious of the Undershadowing of the GREAT LOVE, that wonderful aspect of Divinity expressed by the symbol of the Eagle with its cup-like back, we would again take flight to the Planes of Heaven and be nourished there.

※ ※ ※

UR Journey is one in
which the WHOLE of
our life is involved.
We endeavour, gently,
and with no sense of
strain, to remember
this wholeness, and
hold the memory of it
in our consciousness.

✻ ✻ ✻

N OUR Journey we shall find that, because of our natural and beautiful bond with all the Creatures, it is no longer our wish or need to take their lives for food, or for any purpose. We and they will be greatly helped by this. Indeed, until we cease taking their lives, Peace cannot come on Earth. As our Younger Brethren they too receive the Redeeming influence of Peace River; they too have their Journey. These Journeys will be mutually helpful.

※ ※ ※

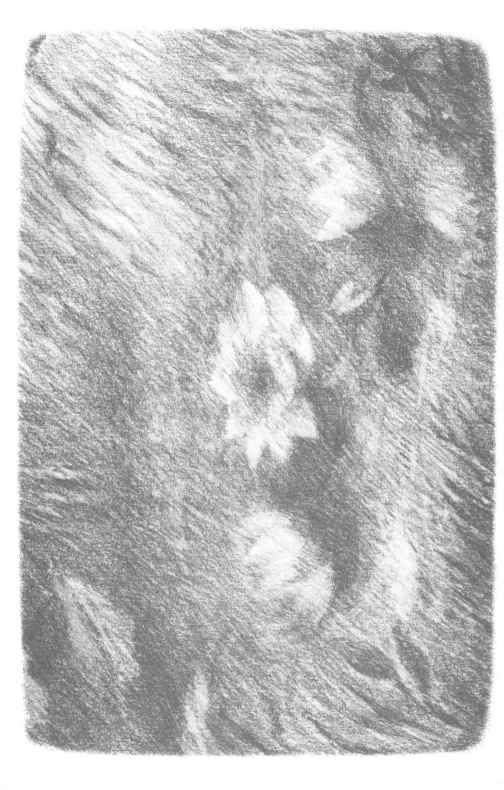

EAR Heavenly ONE,
CREATOR of the vast
Universe and the tiny
flower; CREATOR of all
things beautiful, and
FASHIONER of our own
Being; we essay in
this hour to remember
THY Loving-kindness.

✳ ✳ ✳

HOU hast never forgotten us. We ask that THY Hand now touch us unto the remembrance of THY Love, for it enfolds the whole of our Life. It enfolds both that which we think of as inner, and that which we believe (often erroneously) to be merely outer. We would recognise that they are, in THY sight, one. We would endeavour to realise this.

URTHER, that which we are apt to think of as up and down are, in the truly Mystic sense no more up spatially than they are to left or right, behind, below or in front of. They are only upward and inward in the sense that they are concerned with the Inner Room or Lodge of Man's Being where the Holy Presence dwells, that Presence Who, when realised, permeates the whole of our life.

✻ ✻ ✻

UR Souls have been asleep for many Ages. When they begin to awake we are bemused, and, like one 'coming to' after an anaesthetic, do strange things. We are well if we remember this, for otherwise there will be a tendency to judge amiss. Because it is very painful, this spiritual reawaking, we ourselves, and others, even the misnamed inanimate things we use on earth, will kick against just that very balm which would best bring healing.

※ ※ ※

e ENDEAVOUR to be full of compassion and all those other heavenly graces which help Souls arise and endure the awaking. In the deepest and truest sense we are never parted from the heavens once we have remade the link, the link of which the heavens never lost sight.

✺ ✺ ✺

HROUGH the intercession of the Divine Love on our behalf we have glimpsed again something of the Beauty of the Inner Sanctuary of our Being. We have also felt again the healing atmosphere of God's Presence with us. Thus has our outer life become more meaningful, for we are more AWARE. The Vision given us has shown that ONLY from the innermost can true inspiration come. Also, when applied in every court of our experience, it is that alone can cause truly sensible and practical decisions be made.

HEY who love and cherish us, those heavenly Ones with whom we commune upon the way, help us keep our link in good repair. It is comforting to know that they, and our own Angel, are much stronger than we are. In one sense this is how our weakness can be turned to a strength, provided we can find the willinghood to listen!

✣ ✣ ✣

ONSIDERING further the faculty of true criticism. This may not yet be polarised, and therefore tend to go off at a tangent at the wrong things and in the wrong way. Until it is fully healed it is better that we do not use it at all, relying solely upon the Compassion of the DIVINE LOVE to heal both ourselves and those we love and cherish.

❧ ❧ ❧

HUS we would dwell upon the experience of the LAMB of GOD which taketh away the sins of the world, —that is to say, the direct intervention of the GREAT LOVE for us, in the Act of World rescue.

✳ ✳ ✳

e ENDEAVOUR to become more aware of Love's sacrifice in this Act inviolable in which absolute conse-cration was present. Our part in the Rescue could be manifold; it could also be that we are asked simply to be on Earth to do one very tiny, apparently insignificant deed.

※ ※ ※

OLLOWING our time of quiet and apartness we are well to remember that, notwith-standing our solicitude on parting from our earth tasks and friends there may have been regrets, misun-derstandings, even misjudgements. In our reapproach we may meet these. We ask that the insense of our coming waft on before. Indeed, our patient Angel is ever our van-guard. It is a help when we remem-ber this even though, sometimes, we find his promptings vexatious!

※ ※ ※

UR gratitude for both
heaven and earth will
reach these situations
into which we have to
carry the Love. They
will be aware of its
coming, and there will
be opportunity for true
mutual benefit.

UR Journey back to the Homeland, which together we are taking, has already had its good effects upon the life; and we have, through our sojourning upon the Planes of Heaven, been refreshed and rejuvenated. These have had a hallowing effect upon our everyday tasks. Indeed, in the degree in which we have appropriated and assimilated our spiritual nourishment, these tasks have become one with the heavenly.

❧ ❧ ❧

e HAVE discovered that one of the most helpful things we can do for each other is to recognise the good and the strength and remember one another by these. For these are the things which, when thus remembered, enable us to rise to our best and even beyond it. The DIVINE GOODNESS thus recognised and, like a glowing ember, fanned to stronger warmth, is just that which not only gives strength to rise, but to remain risen; also to deal with the Evil.

※ ※ ※

HE purpose of true Pacifism is to negative the causes and effects of evil, replacing them with the Divine Goodness and the Spirit of a genuine Understanding. It amounts to the total absence of contention, combined with a profound desire for mutual understanding. It is the healing this world needs. For, even now, we can become channels of the Divine Love through whom He will speak to the storm-tossed elements and cause them to obey Him.

※ ※ ※

e MAY be finding that the Streams of Divine Healing into which we have been able to move are helping the one-time falsely critical mind to regain something of its pristine balance, so that, guided by Love's wise hand, it can begin to find again its true place in the wholeness of Life.

❧ ❧ ❧

T IS interesting to note that the word critic comes from an ancient Hellenic word meaning a judge. The true judge within the Soul system is the divider and separator of good from evil. We shall be aided by it in its redeemed state as we seek to recognise in life the principle that all error is truth turned awry; and that evil exists only as the inversion of good.

✳ ✳ ✳

e ASK that the DIVINE GRACE so fill us that, as true tools of the Risen Christ, we can triumphantly meet all things unlovely with the salve of DIVINE LOVE in our hearts, and the balm or balsam of love's fragrance around us.

ow good it is to recognise the Divine Comedy in life's situations! The true balm we endeavour to carry down the heavenly hillsides and give to both our own and others' bruised parts, will become more and more a living part of us, and cause false masks fall away. Barm is of levity, balm of healing. Together they bring the solace of laughter and tears to our side.

✳ ✳ ✳

e RECEIVE the benefits of heaven's balm best as we simply become channels of it. Now, and in the future, to refer to one another as barmy, or balmy, will be well taken!—a mark of recognition and gratitude for the fact that the Streams of Divine Healing are being conveyed to Souls.

✳ ✳ ✳

HE blessing of these healing streams has been richly poured upon us. As the water-lily on the bosom of the lake opens to the kiss of the Sun, so, on the bosom of the Great Deep, the Soul opens to the Kiss of her LORD.

✵ ✵ ✵

HE lily of the lake closes her petals before the Sun sets, and receives the blessing of the cool dews of eve‑ning. The Soul, having bathed in the Sunshine of GOD's Healing Streams, is wise to close her inner doors, there to conserve the Balm. She then comes forth fortified into life and the freshening of the renewed Earth's rising Dews.

ENVOI

HE Joy overflowing from our Cup is filled with the Praise of the MOST HIGH. It is the rhythmic motion of our Being Praising HIM. Praising HIM through showering upon the Earth the unspeakable, the illimitable, the unquenchable Joy, expression of our Love Children of the All-Loving the All-Wise ONE!

IFe moves musically.
Through all its innumer-
able complexities and
complexities of many relationships,
myriad toned, myriad hued, Life,
like the wonderful Music which
made it, moves at last to the
Great Unison, the Great Union
and Oneness within the single
Tone:—and then, that SILENCE
comes, in which the echo of all
that has been, all that is, and all
that will be is heard. For this is
the Realm of Everlasting Peace,

the Source and Fountain-head of
Peace River.

BOOK IV

FLOWERS

BY

PEACE
RIVERSIDE

Y THE fragrant roses in the garden, by the gold-cupped water-lily riding the waters of the breeze stirred pond; we hear the call, the Angels' Call from the Golden Age. The zephyrs whisper it among the osiers by the waterside. The great mountain pines whisper it too. The titmice playing in the fir tree catch the mirth of it; and there is an echo borne within the robin's many songs.

EACE River flows on. In her depths the mysteries of Stars and Man are reflected. Yet more. The very substance and essence of which they are fashioned are found in her. She reflects them because she and they are one. Peace River flows on in so far as we allow her through our lives, and makes us WHOLE.

e ARE the River and the Stars. We are, too, the Mystic Trees who stand upon her banks. That is to say, we have to again become them.

F EVERYTHING we have
ever known our Angel,
our very own OWN
Angel, can remind us.
He is constantly and
ever with us. When we
remember him he can
ALWAYS help us, in so
far as we will allow
him.

UT from the world's turmoil we would make our Approach to HIM, the ONE Who, in HIS Image, made us. We would remember that He made us in the form of the Cross, the symbol of HIS Love and Wisdom, upright, balanced, living, vibrant with HIS Mystery. We would remember HIS Loving-kindness to us. It is with us always.

e is with us NOW, and doth nourish our Soul. From the high Heavens doth He cause the Manna of the Gods to be given us. Its flow to us is unceasing.

We pause, and in the stillness, allow the heavenly ministering Ones to bless us for HIM, He Who is to us the Eternal ROCK of AGES.

LOWERS BY PEACE RIVERSIDE

Flowers are thoughts. They are
the thoughts of Angels. When we
think noble peaceful thoughts,
they make beautiful flowers in the
atmosphere around us; fragrant
flowers.

O we sometimes doubt what we cannot see? Yet there are many things we take for granted that we see not in everyday experience. How about the air we breathe, or the wind that blows and freshens us? The child sees not the streams of love ever flowing to it from its Mother's bosom, yet nestles there. The heart sees not the atmosphere in a room which quiets or disquiets it. Yet these things are tangible; they are real. The air when it is frosty tingles our skin. The effect of the wind we see as trees sway to it and have their roots made strong. And what are we to say of love? We know very well that when we see another through a halo of love we see all the beauty, the truth, the goodness of that one—and I do not mean simply looking through rose-tinted spectacles!—for this experience is real, and we all know it. We have also seen the reverse. A similar experience meets us with Truth. If we look at one whom the world adjudges a criminal with TRUTH in our heart, we see him or her FIRST as a Child of GOD. Later we may need to look with love and understanding on error or mistakes. But the truth shows us Divinity first. Always would our prayer be that we see nobility, Godlikeness first, both in ourselves, however inadequate we may feel, and in others.

e ARe Children of Heaven. Let us remember this. Remember that, however faltering we are, however halt, there ever is that good bit of us, and of others who may vex us. It is ALWAYS there; ever has been and ever will be. Of course we have to put mistakes and error right. It is by our remembrance of Good we do this, NOT by dwelling on Evil. Do we doubt it? Cast the doubt away! Do we tend to look on the dingy side? See the colour

in life, rejoice in its tiniest glimmer
and fan that to a glowing flame!
The dullest pebble seen through
water has a radiance.

ATER is a symbol of
Truth. When we look
at things with a real
living Godfound Truth
in our heart they
radiate.

s I WRITE, the spring is coming. I look in to our little pond, and, rising toward me from its depths are two lily leaves, red like the Kentucky Maples. The Spring of a new life is stirring within us. Do we not feel it? Do we give our good Angel a fair chance to win through to us, and enable us to radiate like her, like him?

T IS good to remember and know now in this hour that the Heavenly Hosts are with us. Ensphering us, and ministering to us, they are with us continually. Very specially is this so as we meet, joining together in our desire to be nearer our Heavenly FATHER. We seek to leave awhile our outer tasks. Those appointed to meet with us come near. They help us in so far as they may without taking from us our own responsibilities. Our

particular responsibility in this
hour is to

RESPOND

to the heavenly
influences as these play upon us.
To allow ourselves to be lifted up,
and to partake of the nourishment
of heaven.

Nourishment needs a pause for its
assimilation. This is true on all
levels of experience. As we dwell
on the Mystery of Life we ask
that the nourishing atmospheres

surround us and enable us to
partake, absorb, assimilate and
make true use of the sustenance
given us.

TRENGTHENED, renewed, enriched; made again WHOLE, resilient and buoyant for service, we ask, ere we go forth, the heavens' blessing on our ways, for we would remember their loving-kindness to us in this hour, and be willing to carry it into our fields of service.

HAVE heard it said, gold-fish in a glass tank give peace to a room. Although we have no fish in our pond, I find that simply gazing into the water brings stillness. If we allow ourselves to thus gaze into the still waters within us—and we do have to be willing to recognise that they ARE there—we find, gradually, there comes the assurance that, above the outwardly increasing maelstrom there is the Hand that guides, the Hand that stills. It is

important we allow ourselves to
recognise —to re-know —to
become again AWARE.

HE Healing Streams, which ever flow from the Eternal World through the Sun as a Spiritual Body, are now more intense than they have been for many ages. They call us back to REMEMBER who we were, who we ARE, and what our ministry is. It is not easy. For a very long time indeed we have dwelt in unutterable darkness and magnetic chaos. We are called out of and up from these conditions, and know the Call is utterly irresistible, all compelling, and is so wonderful in its magnetic pull to the 'good' parts of us that if we ALLOW it, it will take us to the Bosom of HIM Whose POWER it is. To obey with alacrity now in this Day is expected, with sure-found reason, of us all. Almost too wonderful to believe that, in a Cosmic sense, very soon we shall be lifted above the hells in which we have dwelt; lifted above, NEVER to be dragged down into them again. O yes, we may be, shall be, asked to go down to heal them.

Once we allow ourselves to
RESPOND, the upsurging pull of the
Redemption will carry us to where,
gradually,commensurate with our
willinghood, we shall be so
strengthened and renewed that we
can return here and be useful. All
this can happen, is happening to
us, as we rise in our hours of deep
inward prayer and worship. It is
happening to us as we walk the
thoroughfares of life. For these
inward processes are most intimately connected with our outer

everyday activities, conversations, work, play, problems, overcomings, stumblings, recoveries, failures, triumphs;—just everything will again become uplifted, corrected, and form a true part of the whole-ness of life, and its glorious Paean of Praise of the MOST HIGH ONE.

T is not difficult to see that Man is a seeking Being. It is when he begins to seek a reason for his being HERE that he finds even the wonderful mental powers inadequate. And why? Because they are of earth, however miraculous. They of themselves can never tell us of our origin. The mind, alone on the waters of life, distraught and storm-bound, is given directive by the Voice Who rides ABOVE the waves. This is so even in human terms. I myself have been 'brought to' by a human voice from a stable vessel at sea when I was storm-tossed, and given directive. The Voice of GOD speaks above the storm, and, because we ARE HIS Children we CAN hear it. Indeed, He it is Who in HIS Divine FATHERHOOD MOTHERHOOD of us enables us to rise and sing again:

"O Love that wilt not let me go,
. . . .
I give THEE back the life I owe,
That in THINE ocean depths its flow
May richer, fuller be."

What depths are these of which
the poet Matheson speaks? Depths
within us?

S IT noble to serve? Is it MORE noble to serve a great cause though one becomes oneself but a tiny drop in its ocean; or lord it oneself over oneself? It is hard, oh so hard for the mind with all its wonderful powers to realize that its supreme attainment, its supreme goal is to be simply a servant of that greater power within us we name the Soul. That this, after all the thousands of years in an earth historic sense of the growth of the intellect, is to

be its supreme end, simply to be a
servant is—yes, it is hard! But
this is only the beginning! When
we find our glimpse of a life above
and beyond this earthly sojourn
growing into a vista at first limited
but by and by expanding with a
view back to the sunset hues
Aeons prior to that "long long ago"
of which archeology tells us, in
that slowly emerging memory of
the Golden Age, that time when
our lives were full of joy reflected
from Angel faces—it is hard to

look glum when a child smiles upon one! —that memory which our yearning brings, however imperceptibly, nearer and clearer, then we know that even the Soul's governance of our many powers is but a delegated one. She herself with all the memories of vast Aeons upon Aeons of Ages built into the very fabric of her Being is, with all her true greatness, yet but a tiny Child-Servant to the FATHER-MOTHER. With her age, so her Childlikeness grows.

UR prayers ᴀʀᴇ heard. We are wise if we do not confine ourselves to asking for little things. The Soul is great. Great will be the joy in the Heavens at her full awaking. Great will her inheritance be. Great will her power be to serve for Gᴏᴅ through all obedient venues. Fʀᴇᴇ ʙᴇᴄᴀᴜꜱᴇ ᴡɪʟʟɪɴɢ ᴛᴏ ʙᴇ ᴏʙᴇᴅɪᴇɴᴛ ᴛᴏ ᴀ ʜɪɢʜᴇʀ ᴄᴀʟʟ. The world at her best moments, the best moments of her noblest Children, has seen these things, has acted

upon them in so far as, in the half-
dark spiritually smogridden circumstances was possible. Now, in these
days, like the athletes in a relay,
we take the lighted torch from the
past and carry it forward. There is
this difference. There is a difference
of LEVEL; for we now have to rise
in consciousness to the level of the
Soul, and LIVE there, not simply
glimpse from afar. There is the difference of light. That light which,
perforce, had to suffice through
the Dark Ages—and I mean the

Spiritually Dark Ages, not merely a few hundred years of pre-Medieval history—that torch which, thanks be, kept us going then, what is it to become? At what Altar, from what 'glowing stone' are we now to take its ray? It must be like the source of the river, high up where the air is pure where the expanding view is far flung. It is here, both inwardly and outwardly, refresh-ment is to be found. It is here the Soul may spread her wings and fly. It is here on Earth the Eagle dwells.

It is here in the experience of the Soul her eagle powers of heaven-ward flight are found, those wonder-ful powers within us by the use of which we may safely and surely rise above the maelstrom and find peace. It is here we regain our power to soulicly look into the Sun; also rise above the evil, yet then take and transmute it, for that is what our spiritual talons are for, to carry the evil up and away. We then have given to us that wonderful Godlike power with

which, when we are so directed by
HIM, we can change hate back to
Love, Evil back to good, sorrow
back to that Divine Joy which will
buoy us heavenward to take up
again the Golden Age Heritage that
awaits us. Thus re-equipped for
service here on Earth, we will go
into the world and heal it. Not of
ourselves can we do this; only in
so far as we are Channels of the
mighty on-rushing flow of the
Living Waters of GOD's Love can
we act.

AY we be willing, willing to be and do, right here and now. May we be trusting. May we be filled with trust. May we be filled with a wise love and a loving giving; a Joy that is not of this Earth, for it comes from GOD Who is above the Earth but expects us as the Channels of it to bring it into the Earth-life HERE. That is why we are here. Everything we touch and do, think and say, feel purpose and desire;— in EVERYTHING must be carried that

Love, that precious Talisman which
is the very Presence of God our
Father-Mother with us always.
There is nothing, absolutely nothing
in our life that cannot be touched
by Him.

NEEDFUL part, a central part of the Promise of Life is that, gradually, we will be willing and able to allow the GREAT LOVE to enfold us utterly, and, enfolding to permeate; then involute through us unto perfect Manifestation of HIMSELF in Life.

es, it is there, the realm of beauty's origin, that beauty which abides. The transient Earth-beauty is a wonderful echo of it. When we find ourselves in situations where beauty seems absent, perhaps absent in thought and feelings as well as surroundings, it is a help to remember, and endeavour to abide in the remembrance, that the abiding Beauty is omnipresent; is with us always.

UR compassion flows to all who find it difficult to abstain from alcohol and drugs. These give false elation. The Soul, seeking to rise above the deadness of this Earth, is tempted; for both give speedy, if superficial and temporary, release. Prayer, desire for the flight of the Spirit to take us TRULY above Earth's leaden deadness, is the unfailing cure. Never would we sit in judgement. Rather would we endeavour to generate an atmosphere of joy and

upliftment. It is possible to show
in our life the results of aspiration,
and that this makes us truly
spiritually 'high.'

e of good heart! Be great of heart! The Calm cometh in which He alone dwells. The Haven beckons and draws thee, Soul of Light, Soul whose Life spans back to its origin in the Eternal World, and on to its fulfilment of His Promise Ages hence. Forget the littleness, the smallmindedness, the fainthearted-ness. Know thyself, KNOW thyself again beautiful strong and true, full of a glad hope and joyful purpose. Filled again with that PERFECT

TRUST which gives tranquility and complete assurance. Know thyself GOD's Child, and TRUST HIM.

AFTERWORD

e BEGAN this little book
with the words Blessing
and Heaven, given and
shared, and TRUST. This AFTERWORD
carries us from the innermost
where together we have dwelt,
with the riches we have gathered
there, into the outermost courts
where we would continue to dwell
with the PRESENCE of GOD and
hold the riches Sacred in their

APPLICATION.

EAR Heavenly FATHER-
MOTHER! Most Loving,
most Wise One! May we
know THee yet more fully in this
hour as our Lover and our King!
May we be enabled in every act to
make of our WHOLE life a Holy
Communion in Union with THee,
and in exposition of the Sacred
Mystery of Being in service for
THee!

O BLESS is good. To be blessed is to be aware of an all-pervading, all-enfolding Love. The laying on of hands is symbolic. For one in touch with the inner worlds it can be a way of conveying the streams of Peace River to Souls. There are many, many ways. As we are prepared, hour by hour, day by day for the Work which lies ahead, we shall prayerfully become aware of our little niche and simply occupy it. In His Ways there is no fuss, no hesitation. He gently, firmly, draws us to HIMSELF and enables us to become again like HIM. That is the blessing He ever holds for us. It is HIMSELF He gives us, and bids us know HIM as our FATHER and MOTHER in One.

LOVE DIVINE! THOU dost ensphere the lives of ALL THY Children, every-where. We would grow into the consciousness of our Childhood to THEE, that it pervade every stage in life's grand processional. It is THY gift to us. As THY blessing rains upon us we lift up our Cup, and ask that THOU make us worthy suitors for THY Love, and fit Channels for the wise distribution of it through life's ways.

S Thou Blessest us,
Thy Peace River
flows through us
in blessing to all
Souls.

"Peace! Let there be stillness. And there was the Great Silence in which the winds and the waves grew Calm."

Words by J. Todd Ferrier.